Bison

my favorite animal

I0884240

Published in the United States of America by Cherry Lake Publishing
Ann Arbor, Michigan
www.cherrylakepublishing.com

Reading Adviser: Marla Conn MS, Ed., Literacy specialist, Read-Ability, Inc.
Book Design: Jennifer Wahi
Illustrator: Jeff Bane

Photo Credits: © Malgorzata Litkowska / Shutterstock.com, 5; © Greg and Jan Ritchie / Shutterstock.com, 7; © KSwinicki / Shutterstock.com, 9; © Images by Dr. Alan Lipkin / Shutterstock.com, 11; © Sekar B / Shutterstock.com, 13; © David Osborn / Shutterstock.com, 15; © Alessandro Pierpaoli / Shutterstock.com, 17; © Bryant Aardema / Shutterstock.com, 19; © AndreAnita / Shutterstock.com, 21; © Helen's Photos / Shutterstock.com, 23; © Ozerina Anna 2-3, 24; Cover, 1, 8, 12, 20, Jeff Bane

Copyright ©2018 by Cherry Lake Publishing
All rights reserved. No part of this book may be reproduced or utilized in any form or by any means without written permission from the publisher.

Library of Congress Cataloging-in-Publication Data has been filed and is available at catalog.loc.gov

Printed in the United States of America
Corporate Graphics

table of contents

About the author: Dr. Virginia Loh-Hagan is an author, university professor, former classroom teacher, and curriculum designer. She's eaten bison meat before. She didn't care for it. She lives in San Diego with her very tall husband and very naughty dogs. To learn more about her, visit www.virginialoh.com.

About the illustrator: Jeff Bane and his two business partners own a studio along the American River in Folsom, California, home of the 1849 Gold Rush. When Jeff's not sketching or illustrating for clients, he's either swimming or kayaking in the river to relax.

looks

Bison are big. They can be 6 feet (2 meters) tall. They can weigh up to 2,000 pounds (907 kilograms). They have a large head. They have a hump on their back. It helps them move through snow. They have **hooves**.

They have horns. Their horns are bent. They are sharp. They can be 2 feet (61 centimeters) long. They use the horns to fight.

Bison have long fur. They have a long **beard** and **mane**. Their fur is brown. It is dark. It is thick.

home

Bison live in North America. They live on **plains**. Plains have open spaces. They like having lots of land. They are the biggest animals in North America.

Many years ago, people hunted bison. Too many bison died. They needed help. Now, many bison live in big parks. They are safe there.

food

Bison eat plants. In the winter, plants can be hard to find. They must dig under snow. They find grass and **twigs**.

A bison's stomach has four parts. They eat. The food comes back up. They chew it again. This is called chewing their cud.

Bison **wallow**. They dig in the ground. They make holes. They roll in the mud and dirt. This keeps flies away. It helps them **shed**.

Bison swim well. They can run fast. They run up to 35 miles (56 kilometers) an hour. They live in herds. They don't like being alone. They **roam**. They can travel far.

Bulls are males. **Cows** are females. Herds are all bulls or all cows. In the summer, they come together to **mate**.

glossary & index

glossary

beard (BEERD) hair that grows on the chin area

bulls (BULZ) male bison

cows (KOUZ) female bison

hooves (HOOVZ) the hard parts that cover the feet of animals

mane (MAYN) hair that grows on an animal's neck area

mate (MATE) to join together to produce babies

plains (PLAYNZ) large, open, flat areas with few trees and lots of grass

roam (ROHM) to move about in a large area without a goal

shed (SHED) to lose something, such as fur

twigs (TWIGZ) small branches

wallow (WAH-loh) to roll about in mud or dirt

index